Dazaga/Tûbu

Kukurširaã

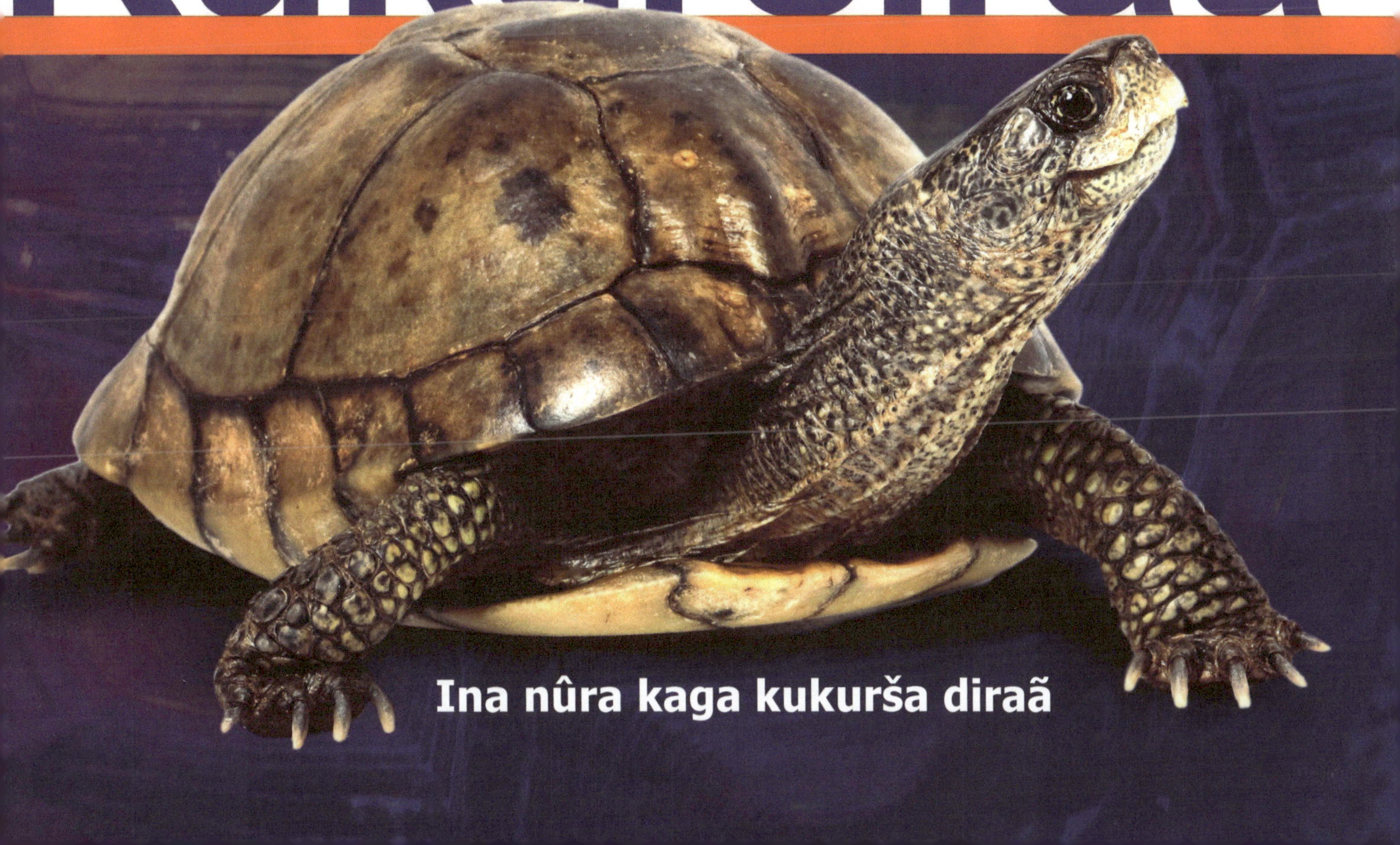

Ina nûra kaga kukurša diraã

Ari

Ari ini orrora ginna ru ŋîla dinare.
Ini lau dîiŋa sowu curunni.

Kôi hêdine kogo buru owon, ciiru dogu danni.

Tiya hunaã šilla ni munta ni.

3

Dûndun

Dûndun mire firi huma kukura buru dîi.

Kôi êyi ciiŋa duro ciki. Ina zira zira hakintoo wirigi.

Awini orrora addiyã addiyã ariya nta bôbolta nta kaga hakintoo wirigi.

5

Kêziŋki

Kêziŋki owa hunaã danara, ini eke addiyoo na daa bîigi.

Kôi gur du ini daa ciiŋa tûrtu tigisigi.

Saa hunaã nunukugi, naana hun nu bî rayiŋi.

Kêziŋki kîñila 160 gor dîi. Kinila gura yaya dîri.

Coromaĩ

Coromaĩ dugusu tiganigi.
Ina gura burayi wugi.

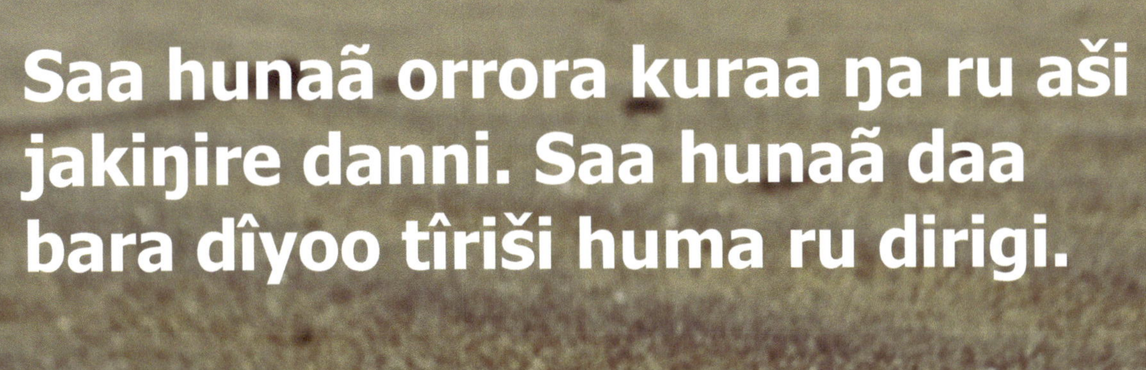

Saa hunaã orrora kuraa ŋa ru aši
jakiŋire danni. Saa hunaã daa
bara dîyoo tîriši huma ru dirigi.

Ini tra firi huma lau dîyoo
firi gor sowere curugi.

9

Lîddi

Lîddi mire ini dîiŋa daa keledinire nusoo girciŋi.

10

Kubbeyinoo durusu huma ba fôu gor tigisigi.

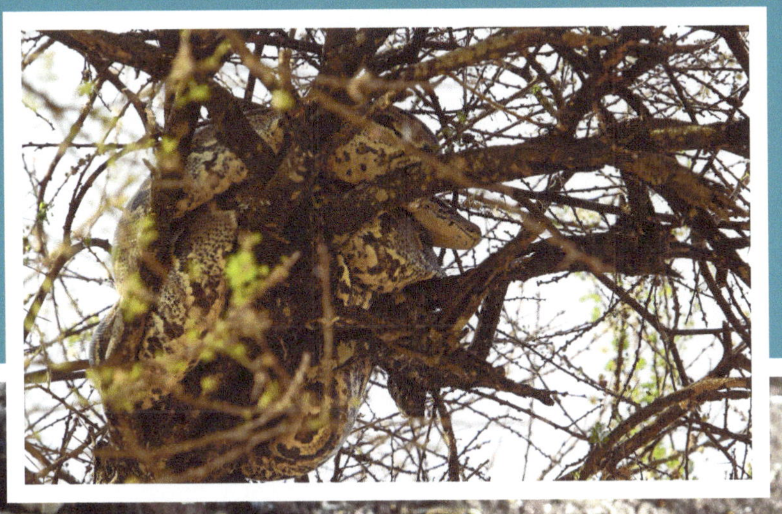

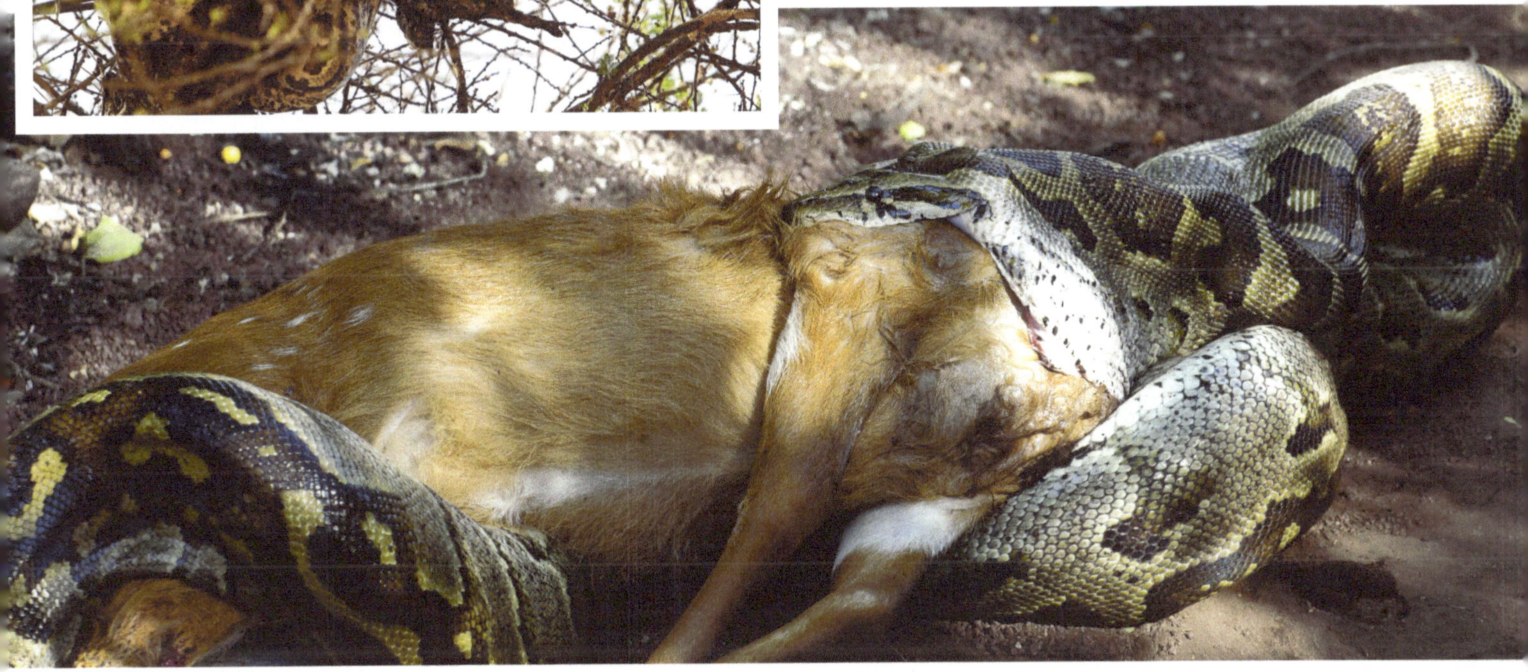

Cî huma kôoši kege lintiŋi. Ini tra cîroo tûkul lu girciŋi. Kîši huma duro yiiŋi. Ini tra kîši huma bu kogo «Kîši lîddi-u yenum» intigi.

Galagala

Êruũ mire bûrru durusu diga ru lôyinire kûila hunaã duro mûugi.

12

«Galagala daa mariĩ» intigi. Daa mara ginna aŋkira. Gura yaliyã huntaã hakintoo wirigi.

Ini tra lau dîgire burayiŋoo nununnoo lau danni, nunuwoo lau dîgi.

13

Koka

Koka mire owor kore. Ina mire kaga duroo kuree ru kii gôogi.

14

Koka owa hunaã buru durusa.
Kasar sonnu. Kôi mire ciiŋa ini tra irrigire kogo daginni.
15

Mogoron

Mogoron ini auzu dirigire kogo ôoši turosere caagi. Firi durusu dîi, hêdine niroo ncaagi.

16

Mura duro guru ŋila
hunaã muncintoo
durusu tigisigi.

17

Aasu

Aasu duruŋoo saa ŋûlli ye gîskei ye ru fartire kogo lîfinne.

Aasa ini tra wirigiroo cagapcintinni gircintigi.

Aasa šîya hunaã aga danne ru bî bazigi.

Ini tra gîri bazigire kogo ca ru gîri bazinni tiliši ru bazigi.

19

Nûru

Nûru yege huma ru kûptire, duro tumusu cii tiganigi.

Gura buru danara adani daa bîyoo goyintu tigantigi. Kûsur huma daa goyi dîi. Nûru guru ginna ŋila 150 gor buzugi.

Nûru fôru ŋa

Nûru fôru ŋa fôruũ
bussu duro tiganigi.

22

Kûila dûrugire burayiŋoo fôruũ cî daa aniši duro jûinere duro wine ru fûrugi.

Tafu duro yala tigisoo curukugi fôruũ duro zutugi.

Diga danni. Ina êfira kaga yûũ duro kamayiŋire dîi.

Seseliye

Seseliye guru na yesku guru na ziri. Aasu kii tûruta ciiru digiyã dîi.

Orrora addiyã ariya kaga wugi.
Sigin aši huma kukuršire ciina addira lowii.
25

Amma geyintiraã: APE ©2017
Amma ruyintiraã: Arumi Mamar, Mamar Bokor, Yîsip Ger and Rivers Camp (Galmai Wûji)
Aũ kêliyima: Robert Johnson (Sûmpi Zen)

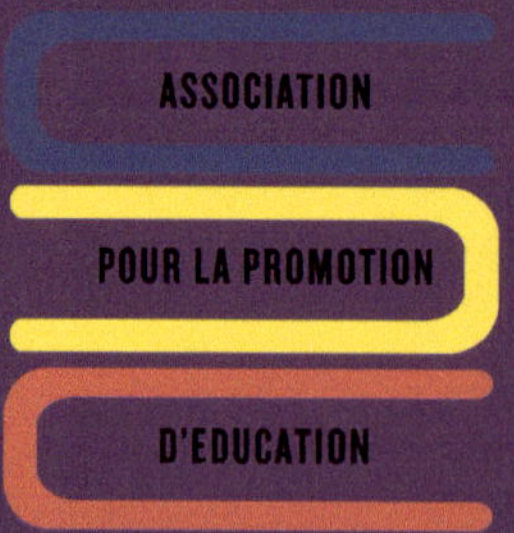